Owls in the Night

CW00665701

Written by Catherine Baker

Collins

Owls perch up high.

They look for food at night.

They zoom down in the dark.

They look for food.

This owl hooks up a fish.

6

sharp talons

fish

Owls need good sight.

They can hear well, too.

They zoom in the moonlight.

They see near and far!

The chicks wait for Mum.

They need lots of food!

Owls

🐾 Review: After reading 🐾

Use your assessment from hearing the children read to choose any GPCs, words or tricky words that need additional practice.

Read 1: Decoding

- Challenge the children to read the /oo/ words. Ask: Which have the /**oo**/ sound as in "book" and which have the /oo/ sound as in "room"?

  look   food   zoom   hooks   good   too

  Ask the children to read the multisyllabic words: **talon**, **moonlight**

Read 2: Prosody

- Model reading each page with expression to the children. After you have read each page, ask the children to have a go at reading with expression.
- On pages 11 and 13 show the children how you add expression to the sentences that end with exclamation marks.

Read 3: Comprehension

- Turn to pages 14 and 15. Ask the children to describe what each picture shows. Can they think of a caption or labels for each picture?
- For every question ask the children how they know the answer. Ask:
  o What do owls look for at night? (*food*)
  o Are they flying about at night or during the day? How do you know? (e.g. *They fly at night because the book says they look for food at night and zoom in the dark.*)
  o What have you learned about owls?